Now That You Are Born Again, What Next?

EMMANUEL ADEWUSI

CCCG Publishing House

Scriptures are taken from the New King James Version. Copyright 1979, 1980, 1982 by Thomas Nelson, Inc. Used by permission. All right reserved.

Author: Emmanuel Adewusi

ISBN: 978-1-989099-64-3 (hardcover)

ISBN: 978-1-989099-65-0 (e-book)

First Printing 2025

Contents

Dedication

To my personal Lord and Saviour, Jesus Christ, you demonstrated excellence in nurturing the apostles to live victorious Christian lives.

To my ever-present Helper, the Holy Spirit. You are the one working through me, enabling me to be and do all that God desires for and of me.

To my wife, Ibukun, for your constant love and tireless support.

To my parents, for nurturing me to become the man I am today.

To everyone who has contributed to my life one way or the other, this book is a testament to your positive impact on my life.

Preface

Have you ever wondered what to do after giving your life to Jesus? Oftentimes, we are so excited about a decision we have made that we do not take time to know what to do next. You might have heard of the term buyer's remorse. This sometimes happens to people who become born again. Many times, they are too guilty to admit that they have or are experiencing this kind of emotion. They are happy and excited about their decision for a while before thinking, "Now That I Am Born Again, What Next?" Is it back to business as usual? Do I need new friends? Should I break up with my unbelieving boyfriend or girlfriend? You know that old things have passed away and all things have become new, but you still do not know the new things to expect and the new things to do.

You may have found yourself around a bunch of Christians who quickly inundate you with a laundry list of things to begin to do. They often forget that a newborn is not yet well-equipped to do certain things. They begin to drown you with Bible verses to memorize, activities to get involved in, spiritual warfare to engage in, and even carnal things to put away; they just want you to live, breathe, and eat Christianity.

This book will serve as a guide to what you can begin to focus on as a new believer. This book will help you focus on the things needed to lay a solid foundation for a victorious Christian life ahead of you.

This book is for new believers, those responsible for teaching or nurturing new believers, and all believers so you can understand how to support your new spiritual family members.

1

The Reality of Your Born Again Experience

I gave my life to Jesus Christ on June 12, 1994 at Lagos State Model College Kankon, a boarding secondary school in Lagos, Nigeria. During a Sunday Service, the fiery preacher painted a picture of where I would go if I did not give my life to Christ. Before I knew what was happening, I ran to Christ as fast as my legs could carry me and surrendered my life to Him. My journey was not the smoothest, as I often stumbled and found myself repenting repeatedly. The more I sinned, the longer it took me to return to Christ. This continued until I travelled outside my home country to Poland. While in Poland, I began to lose taste for the compromises I was making.

I was no longer comfortable in the sinful lifestyles of the past. I started sensing that if I did not change my ways, something terrible would happen to me. I later understood this to be the sanctifying work of the Holy Spirit in my heart. In Poland, I rededicated my life to Jesus Christ and eventually got baptized in the Holy Spirit when I moved to Copenhagen, Denmark.

You might be asking yourself the same questions I asked myself in my early days. How do I know that I am born again? Am I still born again? Why don't I "feel" what I once felt when I first came to Christ? Is there a "feeling" I need to feel? Does everyone feel it? How come I am not feeling it? Am I truly born again? And many other questions. Let's see the Bible's response to these questions.

WHAT DOES IT MEAN TO BE BORN AGAIN?

You are Reconciled with Christ

As Scripture says, *"Now all things are of God, who has reconciled us to Himself through Jesus Christ, and has given us the ministry of reconciliation,"* (2 Corinthians 5:18, NKJV)

You are a New Creation

According to 2 Corinthians 5:17 (NKJV), *"Therefore, if anyone is in Christ, he is a new creation; old things have passed away; behold, all things have become new."*

Your Spirit is Joined with Christ, and You are Now Alive with Him

You died with Christ, and you resurrected with Him. When Adam fell, he was still physically alive, but his spirit lost contact with God's Spirit; hence, the result of the earlier warning that if he ate the fruit in the middle of the garden, he would die.

According to 1 Thessalonians 5:23 and Ephesians 2:4-5, every human comprises spirit, soul, and body. Once you accept Jesus Christ into your heart, the spirit man is re-connected with God's Spirit, and you are now considered spiritually alive with Christ. Spiritual growth begins from taking this step of faith.

What do I Need to do to be Born Again?

In the gospel that Jesus and the Apostles preached, all you need to be born again is to realize that you are a sinner in need of a Saviour (repentance), recognize that God has sent the Saviour, Jesus, to pay for your sins by dying on the cross and accepting Jesus as your Lord and Saviour. This is important to note because some have gone out into the world, convincing people that they do not need to repent of their sins; they only need to believe in Christ, and they will be saved.

It is noteworthy that even though the Bible does not always state that a person repented before they got saved, it is implied that they realized their sinful state and turned around from it by accepting the Lordship of Jesus Christ. In essence, whether you specifically state in your confession that you are repenting of your sins, it must be understood that life in Christ is a new one. Hence, there must be a sincere desire to turn away from the previously sinful life.

To experience the redemptive power of the gospel, you should accept that even though you are a "good person," you are a sinner in need of a Saviour, Jesus Christ. If you accept Christ in your heart without acknowledging your previously sinful nature, it will take a while to experience the redemptive power of the gospel.

A few Scriptures clearly state this doctrine:

- *"Now when they heard this, they were cut to the heart, and said to Peter and the rest of the apostles, 'Men and brethren, what shall we do?' Then Peter said to them, 'Repent, and let every one of you be baptized in the name of Jesus Christ for the remission of sins; and you shall receive the gift of the Holy Spirit."* (Acts 2:37-38, NKJV)

- *"Repent therefore and be converted, that your sins may be blotted out, so that times of refreshing may come from the presence of the Lord,"* (Acts 3:19, NKJV)

- *"To Him all the prophets witness that, through His name, whoever believes in Him will receive remission of sins."* (Acts 10:43, NKJV)

How do I Know I am Now Born Again?

In the world system, seeing is believing. In the system of the kingdom, what God says is what we believe, and then we are empowered to become it. Hence, in the kingdom of God, God says it, we believe it, and then we become it.

God says that once we receive Jesus Christ as our personal Lord and Saviour and confess that He is the Son of God, we become children of God. *"But as many as received Him, to them He gave the right to become children of God, to those who believe in His name: who were born, not of blood, nor of the will of the flesh, nor of the will of man, but of God"* (John 1:12-13) This means that we do not need to feel anything before we believe what God has said.

Sometimes, you may immediately lose taste for your former sinful lifestyle and gain the power to overcome it. In other cases, though you are truly born again, you might still be struggling with a sinful lifestyle. This should not be the litmus test for determining your new spiritual status. All you should go by is what the Word of God has said concerning you in 2 Corinthians 5:17, *"Therefore, if anyone is in Christ, he is a new creation; old things have passed away; behold, all things have become new."* Keep your eyes focused on what God has said, and you will begin to experience the reality of a new life in Christ.

How do I Know I Have Been Truly Forgiven?

As mentioned earlier, man is made up of the spirit, soul, and body. The emotions of guilt originate from the soul and can sometimes be felt in the body. Forgiveness comes from fully believing what God says in 1 John 1:9, NKJV: *"If we confess our sins, He is faithful and just to forgive us our sins and to cleanse us from all unrighteousness."*

To understand forgiveness, you must note that immediately you sincerely ask God to forgive you, according to His word, He will immediately forgive and forget your transgressions.

"For I will be merciful to their unrighteousness, and their sins and their lawless deeds I will remember no more" (Hebrews 8:12)

"I, even I, am He who blots out your transgressions for My own sake; And I will not remember your sins" (Isaiah 43:25)

Mental knowledge of this alone will not suffice in helping you receive forgiveness. Spend enough time meditating on these truths until you fully believe them. Subsequently, you will know throughout your faith journey, that whenever you have sincerely asked God for forgiveness and still "feel" guilty, it does not matter. This is so because God's word is true; it is not based on your false feelings. No matter how grave or minor your sins were, God has promised to forgive you of them once you come to Him in repentance (Psalms 51:17)

2

Remaining a Witness: Baptism and Fellowship with the Holy Spirit

WHO IS THE HOLY SPIRIT?

The Trinity comprises God the Father, God the Son, and God the Holy Spirit. Christians do not serve three Gods but one. God chose to manifest His presence to the world in three ways: as the Father, the Son, and the Holy Spirit. Jesus validated that God is one in Mark 12:29, Jesus replied, *"This is the most important: 'Hear O Israel, the Lord our God is One Lord."*

Even though they are all equal in status (because they are one), at different times in history, one has gained prominence over the other. After Jesus ascended to heaven, the Holy Spirit has become the most important member of the Trinity on the earth today.

People usually do not consider the term "Holy Spirit" a name. Instead, they think of the phrase as a description. Maybe this is because they do not think of the Spirit as a person. People think of Him as an influence, thus giving Him a title, just as people give titles to cars or hurricanes.

His primary name, Holy Spirit, has a twofold implication. First, when we allow the Holy Spirit into our lives, He should make us holy, as His name implies. *"Or do you not know that your body is the temple of the Holy Spirit who is in you, whom you have from God, and you are not your own?"* (1 Corinthians 6:19) Second, when we live by the principles of the Holy Spirit, He will make us spiritually-minded because we become like Him. Hence, you will become holy and spiritually-minded as you enjoy your walk and fellowship with the Holy Spirit.

Before Cornerstone Christian Church of God started, I often asked the Holy Spirit why many Christians were ineffective witnesses in their walk with God. The Lord said, *"It is because many of them are not baptized in the Holy Spirit."* In the early Church, every time a person got saved, they were prayed for to receive baptism in the Holy Spirit. I then resolved to emphasize the significance of baptism in the Holy Spirit as an important prerequisite to being a living, effective witness

BAPTISM IN THE HOLY SPIRIT

Jesus introduced the Holy Spirit to His disciples in John 14:16-17: *"And I will ask the Father, and he will give you another advocate to help you and be with you forever— the Spirit of truth. The world cannot accept him because it neither sees him nor knows him. But you know him, for he lives with you and will be in you."*

On one occasion, he gave them this command in Acts 1:5: *"Do not leave Jerusalem, but wait for the gift my Father promised, which you have heard me speak about. For John baptized with water, but in a few days you will be baptized with the Holy Spirit."*

The promise was fulfilled when the Holy Spirit descended on the thirsty disciples, now Apostles, as they heeded Christ's instructions to tarry in Jerusalem until that promise was fulfilled.

"When the day of Pentecost came, they were all together in one place. Suddenly a sound like the blowing of a violent wind came from heaven and filled the whole house where they were sitting. They saw what seemed to be tongues of fire that separated and came to rest on each of them. All of them were filled with the Holy Spirit and began to speak in other tongues as the Spirit enabled them." (Acts 2:1-4)

Baptism simply means an immersion. Baptism in the Holy Spirit means being filled with the Holy Spirit. This should not be mistaken for being born again. We become born again when we accept that Jesus is Lord. However, from the account in Acts 10, we see that being baptized in the Holy Spirit can happen simultaneously with being born again. We saw this happen in the story of Cornelius.

"There was a certain man in Caesarea called Cornelius, a centurion of what was called the Italian Regiment, a devout man and one who feared God with all his household, who gave alms generously to the people, and prayed to God always. About the ninth hour of the day, he saw clearly in a vision an angel of God coming in and saying to him, "Cornelius!" And when he observed him, he was afraid, and said, "What is it, lord?" So he said to him, "Your prayers and your alms have come up for a memorial before God. Now send men to Joppa, and send for Simon whose surname is

Peter. He is lodging with Simon, a tanner, whose house is by the sea. He will tell you what you must do." (Acts 10:1-6)

Even though Cornelius was devout, he was not born again because he had not heard the gospel of Christ or had the chance to accept Jesus Christ into his heart. The Lord then sent an angel to ask Cornelius to send for Peter. Peter's mission was to preach the gospel to Cornelius and his household so they can believe in Jesus Christ.

"While Peter was still speaking these words, the Holy Spirit fell upon all those who heard the word. And those of the circumcision who believed were astonished, as many as came with Peter, because the gift of the Holy Spirit had been poured out on the Gentiles also. For they heard them speak with tongues and magnify God." (Acts 10:44-46)

The word "heard" in verse 44 means that they received Peter's word concerning Jesus as the Christ. Once that happened, according to John 1:12, they became children of God, thereby, fulfilling the condition to receive the baptism of the Holy Spirit.

In many other instances in Scriptures, including that of the disciples, they became born again before receiving the baptism of the Holy Spirit. This shows that the disciples had received Jesus as the Christ and Lord.

"Then, the same day at evening, being the first day of the week, when the doors were shut where the disciples were assembled, for fear of the Jews, Jesus came and stood in the midst, and said to them, 'Peace be with you.' When He had said this, He showed them His hands and His side. Then the disciples were glad when they saw the Lord. So Jesus said to them again, 'Peace to you! As the Father has sent Me, I also send you.' And when He had said this, He breathed on them, and said to them, 'Receive the Holy Spirit. If you forgive the sins of any, they are forgiven them; if you retain the sins of any, they are retained.'" (John 20:19-23)

Early Converts

Another example is of the early converts receiving Jesus as Lord and being subsequently baptized in the Holy Spirit

"Then Peter said to them, 'Repent, and let every one of you be baptized in the name of Jesus Christ for the remission of sins; and you shall receive the gift of the Holy Spirit. For the promise is to you and to your children, and to all who are afar off, as many as the Lord our God will call.' And with many other words he testified and exhorted them, saying, 'Be saved from this perverse generation.' Then those who gladly received his word were baptized; and that day about three thousand souls were added to them." (Acts 2:38-41)

The Samaritans

The Samaritans in Acts 8 are another example. Acts 8:4-6, shows the people in Samaria accepting Jesus as Lord:

"Therefore those who were scattered went everywhere preaching the word. Then Philip went down to the city of Samaria and preached Christ to them. And the multitudes with one accord heeded the things spoken by Philip, hearing and seeing the miracles which he did." (Acts 8:4-6)

Believers in Samaria

Subsequently, in Acts 8:14-17, it shows those believers in Samaria receiving the baptism of the Holy Spirit:

"Now when the apostles who were at Jerusalem heard that Samaria had received the word of God, they sent Peter and John to them, who, when they had come down, prayed for them that they might receive the Holy Spirit. For as yet He had fallen upon none of them. They had only been baptized in the name of the Lord Jesus. Then they laid hands on them, and they received the Holy Spirit." (Acts 8:14-17)

Paul

Paul received the Holy Spirit when Ananias laid hands on him.

"And Ananias went his way and entered the house; and laying his hands on him he said, 'Brother Saul, the Lord Jesus, who appeared to you on the road as you came, has sent me that you may receive your sight and be filled with the Holy Spirit.' Immediately there fell from his eyes something like scales, and he received his sight at once; and he arose and was baptized." (Acts 9:17-18)

WAYS TO RECEIVE THE BAPTISM OF THE HOLY SPIRIT

By Waiting on the Lord in Prayer and Worship

The disciples waited for the baptism in the Holy Spirit by remaining in prayer.

"Then they returned to Jerusalem from the mount called Olivet, which is near Jerusalem, a Sabbath day's journey. And when they had entered, they went up into the upper room where they were staying: Peter, James, John, and

Andrew; Philip and Thomas; Bartholomew and Matthew; James the son of Alphaeus and Simon the Zealot; and Judas the son of James. These all continued with one accord in prayer and supplication, with the women and Mary the mother of Jesus, and with His brothers" (Acts 1:12-14)

We then saw that the Holy Spirit came upon them in response to their prayers.

"When the Day of Pentecost had fully come, they were all with one accord in one place. And suddenly there came a sound from heaven, as of a rushing mighty wind, and it filled the whole house where they were sitting. Then there appeared to them divided tongues, as of fire, and one sat upon each of them. And they were all filled with the Holy Spirit and began to speak with other tongues, as the Spirit gave them utterance" (Acts 2:1-4)

The disciples were again filled with the Holy Spirit after they prayed.

"After they prayed, the place where they were meeting was shaken. And they were all filled with the Holy Spirit and spoke the word of God boldly" (Acts 4:31)

You wait in prayer and worship by asking God to baptize you in the Holy Spirit. You can pray this prayer in faith:

Heavenly Father, I thank you that I am Your child. I thank You for always answering me whenever I call on You. You promised to give the Holy Spirit to those who ask. Right now, I ask You to baptize me in the Holy Spirit. Thank You, Father, for answering my prayer. In Jesus' name, Amen.

After praying this prayer in faith, begin to praise God and thank Him for the baptism in the Holy Spirit you have received. As you continue in this, I strongly believe that the Holy Spirit will come upon you.

By Laying on of Hands

The baptism in the Holy Spirit can be received through the laying on of hands of someone that is filled with the Holy Spirit. The disciples in Samaria received the Holy Spirit when Peter and John laid hands on them.

"Now when the apostles who were at Jerusalem heard that Samaria had received the word of God, they sent Peter and John to them, who, when they had come down, prayed for them that they might receive the Holy Spirit. For as yet He had fallen upon none of them. They had only been baptized in the name of the Lord Jesus. Then they laid hands on them, and they received the Holy Spirit" (Acts 8:14-17)

Paul received the Holy Spirit when Ananias laid hands on him.

"And Ananias went his way and entered the house; and laying his hands on him he said, 'Brother Saul, the Lord Jesus, who appeared to you on the road as you came, has sent me that you may receive your sight and be filled with the Holy Spirit.' Immediately there fell from his eyes something like scales, and he received his sight at once; and he arose and was baptized" (Acts 9:17-18)

By Listening to an Anointed Message

Cornelius and his household received the baptism in the Holy Spirit while Peter was preaching the gospel to them. Perhaps, God knew that this was the most effective way to demonstrate to the early Church that He was calling the gentiles to be Christians as well.

"While Peter was still speaking these words, the Holy Spirit fell upon all those who heard the word" (Acts 10:44)

EVIDENCE OF THE BAPTISM IN THE HOLY SPIRIT

Speaking in Tongues

The examples referred to from Scriptures clearly show that after the baptism in the Holy Spirit, the disciples of Christ spoke in other tongues. This is in fulfillment of Christ's words concerning this.

"He who believes in Me, as the Scripture has said, out of his heart will flow rivers of living water." But this He spoke concerning the Spirit, whom those believing in Him would receive; for the Holy Spirit was not yet given, because Jesus was not yet glorified." (John 7:38-39, NKJV)

These examples below show us that speaking in tongues is evidence of being baptized in the Holy Spirit.

- *"Then there appeared to them divided tongues, as of fire, and one sat upon each of them. And they were all filled with the Holy Spirit and began to speak with other tongues, as the Spirit gave them utterance"* (Acts 2:3-4)

- *"While Peter was still speaking these words, the Holy Spirit fell upon all those who heard the word. And those of the circumcision who believed were astonished, as many as came with Peter, because the gift of the Holy Spirit had been poured out on the Gentiles also. For they heard them speak with tongues and magnify God"* (Acts 10:44-46)

Demonstrating the Fruits of the Holy Spirit

From Scriptures, we understand that there are virtues that accompany the baptism in the Holy Spirit.

"But the fruit of the Spirit is love, joy, peace, long-suffering, kindness, goodness, faithfulness, gentleness, self-control. Against such, there is no law" (Galatians 5:22-23)

A person who is genuinely baptized in the Holy Spirit will display these virtues in increasing dimensions.

In addition to speaking in tongues and displaying the fruits of the Holy Spirit, the more we walk in the Spirit, the more we will manifest the gifts of the Holy Spirit in supernatural signs and wonders in increasing dimensions.

Remaining Filled with the Holy Spirit

The presence of the Holy Spirit in us is a gift from God (see Luke 11:13, NKJV). You must understand that the gift of the Holy Spirit can be lost. After being filled with the Holy Spirit, there are certain things to watch out for, in order to remain filled.

Avoid Sin

The Holy Spirit can be grieved by persisting in a sinful lifestyle or habit even after convictions from the Holy Spirit. There are many Christians who once knew what it meant to be filled with the Holy Spirit, but because of sin, have since gone astray.

"And do not grieve the Holy Spirit of God, by whom you were sealed for the day of redemption," (Ephesians 4:30, NKJV)

King David acknowledged the possibility of the presence of the Holy Spirit departing from a person in his prayer of repentance after he sinned by committing adultery with Bathsheba and arranging for her husband, Uriah, to be killed in battle.

"Do not cast me away from Your presence, And do not take Your Holy Spirit from me." (Psalms 51:11, NKJV)

Fellowship

The Holy Spirit's presence in us is not to be left dormant. We are to fellowship with Him regularly. We are to have the same kind of relationship that the Apostles had with Jesus Christ while He was on the earth.

"The grace of the Lord Jesus Christ, and the love of God, and the communion of the Holy Spirit be with you all. Amen." (2 Corinthians 13:14, NKJV)

Fellowship with the Holy Spirit can be as simple as asking Him questions. Engage with Him as you would a dear friend. Speak to Him, ask Him those burning questions that you have, pour out your heart to Him, cry and lean on Him when you are confused, and believe in faith that He is there listening. You can also regularly fellowship with Him by praying in the spirit (i.e., praying in your heavenly language). Jesus expressed His confidence in the presence of the Holy Spirit in Him in a profound statement that He made while under persecution.

"And He who sent Me is with Me. The Father has not left Me alone, for I always do those things that please Him." (John 8:29, NKJV)

Based on Christ's statement here, we see that His confidence in God's ever-abiding presence is based on Him being in right standing with God at all times. Being in right standing with God simply means being righteous. This does not mean that you do not make mistakes. It simply means that deliberate efforts are being made by you to live a life that pleases God, and when you are convicted of sin, you repent immediately.

With this confidence, begin to engage the Holy Spirit all through your day and watch as your relationship with Him deepens.

3

Harnessing the Power in the Word

You must understand that the Bible is the Word of God. It was packaged by God for our benefit and it contains the very nature and power of God. The Bible is not a storybook, even though it contains stories. It is mainly the very nature of God expressed in written words. Several Scriptures validate this truth.

Before coming to Christ, you had your way of living that was largely against God's prescribed way of life. You responded to challenges in a particular way, you freely engaged in gossip, hatred, selfishness, outbursts of anger to name a few. Now that you have become born again, it is important for you to begin to learn God's prescribed way of life.

"But you must continue in the things which you have learned and been assured of, knowing from whom you have learned them, and that from childhood you have known the Holy Scriptures, which are able to make you wise for salvation through faith which is in Christ Jesus. All Scripture is given by inspiration of God, and is profitable for doctrine, for reproof, for correction, for instruction in righteousness, that the man of God may be complete, thoroughly equipped for every good work." (2 Timothy 3:14-17, NKJV)

The Scripture is the equivalent of God sitting with you to personally show you His way of living. He expects us to be outstanding. He expects us to stand out and shine His light in a dark world. We can only achieve that by allowing His word to transform our lives.

"And do not be conformed to this world, but be transformed by the renewing of your mind, that you may prove what is that good and acceptable and perfect will of God." (Romans 12:2, NKJV)

CHARACTERISTICS OF THE WORD

The Word of God is the Power of God. The Word of God is the equivalent of having a tutor showing us the way to go in every situation that we face.

"All Scripture is given by inspiration of God, and is profitable for doctrine, for reproof, for correction, for instruction in righteousness, that the man of God may be complete, thoroughly equipped for every good work." (2 Timothy 3:16-17, NKJV)

Without a studious lifestyle, a believer can never grow to understand the power the Word contains.

The Word of God is God

According to John 1, the Word of God was there from the beginning. Since the Word of God is God, it means that the Word of God carries the entire nature of God.

"In the beginning was the Word, and the Word was with God, and the Word was God. He was in the beginning with God. All things were made through Him, and without Him, nothing was made that was made." (John 1:1-3, NKJV)

This shows that God is the architect of everything, not evolution and definitely not science.

The Word of God is Creative

God used His words to create most of the world that we see today.

"In the beginning God created the heavens and the earth. The earth was without form, and void; and darkness was on the face of the deep. And the Spirit of God was hovering over the face of the waters. Then God said, 'Let there be light'; and there was light." (Genesis 1:1-3, NKJV)

This shows that God created everything; the world did not just come into existence. The world was not a result of the big bang or evolution or whatever the scientists are calling it.

The Word of God is Illuminating

Since John 1:1-3 makes us understand that Jesus is the Word, and Ephesians 5:14 states that Christ will give us light, it means that the Word of God is light.

"But all things that are exposed are made manifest by the light, for whatever makes manifest is light. Therefore He says: 'Awake, you who sleep, arise from the dead, and Christ will give you light'" (Ephesians 5:13-14, NKJV)

The Word of God is a lamp to our feet and a light to our path. Psalm 119:105 (NKJV) says, *"Your word is a lamp to my feet and a light to my path."*

The Word of God is Living and Powerful

"For the word of God is living and powerful, and sharper than any two-edged sword, piercing even to the division of soul and spirit, and of joints and marrow, and is a discerner of the thoughts and intents of the heart." (Hebrews 4:12, NKJV)

HOW TO APPROACH THE STUDY OF THE WORD

Your approach to reading the Word of God can either maximize your benefit or act as a sleeping pill. A serious approach will lead to a glorious result. Below, I will highlight three key ways of reading/studying the Word of God. You can begin right away to read the Bible in a way that applies to you. Remember that your approach could be a hybrid of some of these techniques.

Topical or Theme Study

In this approach, you search the Scriptures for passages that speak about the topic you are interested in exploring. For example, you might desire to learn about love, patience, anointing, or other topics. The benefit of this approach is that it makes the Scriptures directly applicable to your life and can be easily applied.

At Cornerstone Christian Church of God, we have themes explored monthly. This helps us to focus our attention and get the best out of that area for that month. I usually encourage those in our ministry to follow the theme in their personal devotion to make the best of it.

Sometimes, it can be challenging to remember what you have been learning for the past few weeks/months/years. Using the topical approach will make it easier to remember what you have been studying and evaluate your personal growth about the topic.

Once you have decided on the topic you would like to explore, search your Bible for all applicable passages (chapters and verses of the Bible) and focus on a verse(s) during your allotted time for Bible study/devotion. Some Bibles contain a topical reference. Otherwise, you could use the internet to search for passages that speak to your topic of interest.

Bible Character Study

Another approach to reading the Bible is to read about Bible characters. This approach allows you to read through most of the Bible since the stories about Bible characters are usually spread across several verses or chapters. Even though this is a good approach, it should be blended with other Bible study styles to benefit maximally from the Scriptures.

Reading about the lives of Bible characters will help you gain wisdom on acceptable and unacceptable ways of living. It will show you the biblical paths to success and paths that do not lead to success. Since reading the biographies of people helps us gain wisdom, Bible character study will help you gain more wisdom and insight than you could have obtained from merely learning from your personal experiences.

For example, you could read about Apostle Paul. The study of his life will take you through most books of the New Testament: how he persecuted the church, how he came to know Christ (his conversion), the letters he wrote to the churches, his mentees and the battles he overcame.

Book by Book Study

The other Bible study approach is to read the Bible sequentially. As a new believer, you must become familiar with certain essential truths about God in the Scriptures.

Certain books in the Bible will make more sense to you as a new believer after you have read other books in the Bible. Hence, it may not be beneficial for a new believer to read the Bible sequentially from Genesis to Revelation. The recommended approach is to start reading from the New Testament. The best start will be the book of John, followed by Matthew, Mark, and Luke. They will introduce you to your Lord and Savior, Jesus Christ. After you finish these four books, you should move on to the Epistles in the New Testament. The Epistles are the letters written to you, the believer. They are written to the church. Examples of the Epistles are Romans, Galatians, Ephesians, etc.

In his book *"In Him"*, Kenneth E. Hagin recommended that you look for all expressions such as "in Christ," "in Him," "in Whom," "through whom," etc., as you read through the Epistles. He also suggested that you highlight those expressions when you come across them. He went on to assert that there are approximately 140 of such expressions, most of which are in the Epistles. Some of these, however, don't exactly tell you something you have "in Christ." For instance, Paul's greeting in one Epistle is, "I greet you in the name of the Lord Jesus Christ." That has the expression "in Christ", but it doesn't tell you anything that is yours because you are "in Christ." You will also find other Scriptures that convey the same message but do not use the specific phrases "in Him," etc. Yet, they tell you who you are, or what you are or what you have because you are "in Christ." Now, when you find these Scriptures—make a note of them. Then, meditate on such Scriptures. Begin to confess them and say with your mouth, *"This is who I am, and this is what I am, and this is what I have in Christ."*

Afterwards, you can proceed to read other books in the Old Testament.

This book-by-book approach will help you encounter the person of Jesus Christ in the New Testament. It will also help you discover your new status as a child of God before reading about other Bible characters and the acts of God.

There are devotionals that can help you read through the books of the Bible within a specified period of time, e.g., 90 days or 1 year.

Now that you know how to study the Bible using these three approaches, it's time to get to work. Happy reading!

4

Locate Your Place in the Body

LOCATE THE BODY

As a new believer, you should understand that you are now part of the family of God. Each Church is a representation of the body of Christ. You must locate the Church family that God wants you to become a part of. Do not fall into the trap of the devil where he convinces people that they do not need to be part of a Church.

In Hebrews 10:25, God tells us not to forsake the gathering of the saints.

"Not forsaking the assembling of ourselves together, as is the manner of some, but exhorting one another, and so much

the more as you see the Day approaching." (Hebrews 10:25, NKJV)

Even lions hunt in a pack. They understand that although they are individually strong, they can command more results collectively by being an active part of a like-minded and same-natured group.

Belonging to a Church family helps you to be under spiritual authority. Every child of God must have a spiritual covering. Even though the early Church was a spirit-filled Church, the covering of the Apostles was vital for their ongoing growth, spiritual nourishment, and protection.

Characteristics of a True Church

- The entire Word of God is believed and being preached

- The love of God is present in the congregation

- The spiritual head of the Church, i.e., the Pastors, are displaying the fruits of the Holy Spirit: love, peace, joy, long-suffering, etc., as listed in Galatians 5:22-23

- The leadership of the Church is submitted to the Lordship of Jesus Christ and the Holy Spirit

- There is a genuine desire to help you grow as a new believer

- The Holy Spirit is present and welcome in the congregation

Ultimately, the Holy Spirit is the one who will lead you to the right Church that He is calling you to become a part of. According to Romans 8:14, the true children of God are those that are led by the Spirit of God. You are expected to pray and ask God to lead you to the right Church. When you get there, watch out for some of the characteristics listed above before you settle into that Church family.

LOCATE YOUR PLACE IN THE BODY

After you locate the Church family to belong to, the next step is to find your place in that Church family. You are uniquely gifted by God. You have a special place in the body of Christ that must be discovered if you are going to be effective in the Kingdom of God. Apostle Paul was led by the Holy Spirit to give some insight into this.

"For as the body is one and has many members, but all the members of that one body, being many, are one body, so also is Christ. For by one Spirit we were all baptized into one body—whether Jews or Greeks, whether slaves or free—and have all been made to drink into one Spirit. For in fact the body is not one member but many. If the foot should say, "Because I am not a hand, I am not of the body," is it therefore not of the body? And if the ear should say, "Because I am not an eye, I am not of the body," is it therefore not of the body? If the whole body were an eye, where would be the hearing? If the whole were hearing, where would be the smelling? But now God has set the members, each one of them, in the body just as He pleased. And if they were all one member, where would the body be? But now indeed there are many members, yet one body. And the eye cannot say to the hand, "I have no need of you"; nor again the head to the feet, "I have no need of you." No, much rather, those members of the body which seem to be weaker are necessary. And those members of the body which we think to be less honorable, on these we bestow greater honor; and our unpresentable parts have greater modesty, but our presentable parts have no need. But God composed the body, having given greater honor to that part which lacks it, that there should be no schism in the body, but that the members should have the same care for one another. And if one member suffers, all

the members suffer with it; or if one member is honored, all the members rejoice with it.

Now you are the body of Christ, and members individually. And God has appointed these in the church: first apostles, second prophets, third teachers, after that miracles, then gifts of healings, helps, administrations, varieties of tongues. Are all apostles? Are all prophets? Are all teachers? Are all workers of miracles? Do all have gifts of healings? Do all speak with tongues? Do all interpret? But earnestly desire the best gifts. And yet I show you a more excellent way." (1 Corinthians 12:12-31, NKJV)

Apostle Paul clarifies that God gifts each believer to perform different tasks. Look inwards to discover the gift God has given to you, and based on that, begin immediately to serve God in that capacity in the Church (local Church and the body of Christ as a whole).

Ask Yourself:

- What do I love to do effortlessly?

- What am I passionate about?

- What would I do for the kingdom of God if I were not paid for it?

If you cannot discover your unique gifting, you can speak to your Pastor, leader or mentor to help you in this process. Remember, everything that God does is excellently done. He never created anyone without a unique gifting. He does not make junk. As you discover His gifts in you, begin to immediately function in that gift and watch yourself grow in leaps and bounds.

5

Seek to Grow

CONNECTING WITH THE WORD

Spiritual growth can be likened to physical growth in many ways. The Bible even likens a new believer to a baby.

"As newborn babes, desire the pure milk of the word, that you may grow thereby." (1 Peter 2:2, NKJV)

From this, we understand that for a new believer to grow, they must desire the Word of God sincerely. This means that a strong desire for the Word of God will enable you to grow as a believer.

Even though we can never be fully mature as believers, God still expects us to grow in our knowledge of Him. Sadly, I have seen some people remain as newborn Christians for as long as five years, while I have also seen some new believers grow very fast. The secret is a sincere desire for the Word of God, among other things. One Scripture that summarizes the focus of a new believer to continually grow is:

"The grace of the Lord Jesus Christ, and the love of God, and the communion of the Holy Spirit be with you all." (2 Corinthians 13:14, NKJV)

You connect with the grace of our Lord Jesus Christ through the Word of God, both written (logos) and revealed (rhema). The Bible tells us that Jesus is full of grace and truth.

"And the Word became flesh and dwelt among us, and we beheld His glory, the glory as of the only begotten of the Father, full of grace and truth." (John 1:14)

The Bible also tells us that Jesus is the Word.

"In the beginning was the Word, and the Word was with God, and the Word was God." (John 1:1, NKJV)

This means that if Jesus is the Word and Jesus is full of grace and truth, the Word of God is also full of grace and truth.

Our continuous growth comes from each encounter with grace and truth from the Word of God. Also from 2 Corinthians 13:14, we see that it is important to grow in the love of God. This includes both our love for God, receiving the love of God, and displaying the love of God to others. Finally, we see in 2 Corinthians 13:14 that we are encouraged to have communion with the Holy Spirit. Communion with the Holy Spirit is enhanced through fellowship in the Word of God, engaging in acts of worship, and devoting daily personal time to ask questions and be taught by Him.

MEASURING SPIRITUAL GROWTH

The growth of a believer is measured by the amount of increase they are experiencing in "being" and "doing." The "being" has to do with our character growth (i.e., our fruits), while the "doing" has to do with the results from our activities (i.e., our works). Some Christians mistakenly focus on one more than the other. Some say that it's not what you do that matters, but who you are. Others place more emphasis on works, saying that it is what you do that matters.

The truth is that God is concerned with both — "who we are" and "what we accomplish." Who we are is the foundation for a lifetime of enduring accomplishments. Jesus spent time with His disciples teaching them and helping them to grow before He saw it fit to send them out to minister to others. It is very easy to get carried away in the world that we live in. Measuring where we stand in these two dimensions and at regular intervals is a healthy practice.

Ways to Measure Growth in Your New Identity:

- Are you still struggling with sin or tempted with the same bad habits you had before coming to Christ? (Romans 6:1-23)

- How much of the fruits of the Holy Spirit are evident in your life? (Galatians 5:22-23)

- Are you able to discern and follow the leading of the Holy Spirit through revelation, knowledge or the instructions from Scriptures? (Romans 8:14)

- How much have you allowed the Holy Spirit to work on the unpleasant aspects of your personality? (Galatians 5:16-18)

Ways to Measure Growth in Your Works:

- Are you diligently pursuing your God-given vision?

- Are you fruitful in soul-winning? (John 15:2)

- Are you actively mentoring others? (Matthew 28:18-20)

- Are you serving diligently in your local Church?

- What is the frequency and quality of the manifestation of the gifts of the Holy Spirit in your life? (1 Corinthians 12:7-11)

- How much are you exercising your authority over the devil? (Acts 10:38)

- How much of your redemptive rights are you enjoying? (Galatians 4:1-4)

The results from this self-assessment should neither weigh you down nor make you proud. Instead, let it encourage you to keep pressing on. The areas you find yourself lacking are an indication of where you should focus your attention, in order to continue growing. The goal is to be like Jesus Christ while here on the earth.

Epilogue

Now that you know the next steps, it is time for you to continue your Christian race unhindered. You are now well equipped to avoid the pitfalls that others fell into. You do not need to be confused about what to do now that you are born again.

I recommend that you read the book *"New Creation Realities"* by E. W. Kenyon. It will further enlighten you about the truth of your new position in Christ.

I pray that God will keep you strong till the very end. You will not be a casualty along the way. I pray that the grace to stay strong till the end rests upon you in Jesus' name. You will keep soaring higher and your steps will not be hindered by evil forces in Jesus' name (Amen).

Contact the Author

I know without a doubt that this book has been a blessing to you. I am looking forward to hearing your testimony.

You can stay connected with me through the following platforms:

Instagram: e.adewusi | **Youtube:** Emmanuel Adewusi
Website: emmanueladewusi.org

Review the Book

A Sinner's Prayer

Dear Heavenly Father,

I come to You in the Name of Jesus Christ.

You said in Your Word, "Whosoever shall call upon the name of the Lord shall be saved." (Romans 10:13) I am calling on Your Name, so I know You have saved me now.

You also said that "if you confess with your mouth the Lord Jesus and believe in your heart that God has raised Him from the dead, you will be saved. For with the heart one believes unto righteousness, and with the mouth, confession is made unto salvation." (Romans 10:9-10) I believe in my heart Jesus Christ is the Son of God. I believe that He was raised from the dead for my justification, and I confess Him now as my Lord and Savior.

Thank you, Lord, because now, I am saved!

Thank You, Lord, because I know you have heard my prayer. Thank You, Lord, because I am now born again.

Signed _____

Date _____

About the Author

Apostle Emmanuel Adewusi is the Founding and Lead Pastor of Cornerstone Christian Church of God.

Called into ministry with the mandate to "bring restoration and transformation to all by teaching, preaching, and demonstrating the Gospel of Jesus Christ," he is passionate about seeing lives restored and transformed as God intended from the beginning of creation. He has a zeal for the full counsel of the Word of God, fellowship with the Holy Spirit, and being under spiritual authority.

He authored the books *"The Blessings of Being Under Spiritual Authority," "A Disciplined Life," "The Enlightened Believer," "The Skilled Sower,"* and other impactful titles. He has also released an album titled *"Divine Encounter"* and many more on the way.

Emmanuel Adewusi is joyfully married to his wife, Ibukun Adewusi, and together, they are building a thriving Christ-centered family.